"Don't Heal Me!
I'm on Disability Benefits"

William Timmerman, PhD

"Don't Heal Me! I'm on Disability Benefits"

2022

Pen Shop Publishing

San Antonio, Texas

William Timmerman, PhD

Table of Contents

Introduction

The title "Don't Heal Me! I'm on Disability Benefits" comes from the punch line in a great joke that will come later. If you lived with a physical disability like I have for over sixty years now, you might rightly ask if Jesus could heal you of your physical disability would you seek him out in healing event in your church if he was there tonight? My answer would be, "No". Wonder if Jesus was coming down the aisle would I duck or hide from him? "Nope". I would motion him to come my way not to heal me from my physical disability but from my sinfulness.

I'm a lot like Joni Eareckson Tada. She claimed that a diving accident when she was seventeen leaving her a quadriplegic in a wheelchair was a "glorious intruder", the best thing that ever happened to her. She believes God used it to get her attention and direct her thoughts toward Him. However, it took nearly two years before she arrived at that point after suffering through anger, depression, bitterness, suicidal thoughts, and religious doubts.

I was totally enjoying the summer as a baseball pitching stud in a semi-pro league and celebrating life to the fullest when it all came to a screeching halt on August 8, 1958, just after my twenty-second birthday. That night I gulped down a whole bunch of sleeping pills which had belonged to my grandmother before she died. I had to take them because I felt non-stop, excruciating pain in both my legs like a whole herd of charley horses had run over me. I could not stand, sit, or lie down without cringing in pain. It stayed at a constant "ten" on the pain scale. The sleeping pills did not faze me so the next morning, half stumbling down the outside stairs, I headed to the emergency room. They put me in an isolation ward with the diagnosis of polio. Early on both my arms were paralyzed. With time they got better but I remain paralyzed from the waist down to this day.

This one night in the hospital I awoke to a streak of white flying by me into the room next door while strange alarm sounds were going off. The guy in the room next to me had polio and was in an iron lung. The iron lung had stopped its rhythmic droning sound. He was a 28-year-old man, married with two small children. I had become used to the droning sound of the iron lung that I knew kept him breathing. It wasn't very long until the doctors and nurses walked slowly passed my door with their heads down. I called one of the nurses into my room to find out what was going on. She looked at me with tears in her eyes and said, "He died" then turned around and walked out. As I lay in my bed big tears began to well up in me. It became instantly clear to me the seriousness of what just had occurred. The young man in the room next to me died from polio and I've got polio too! I began to bawl like a baby and pleaded to God to not let me die. I then offered a bargain to God. If he would save me, I would change my life and do good things for him.

Through the years I have tried to live up, at least somewhat, to my part of the bargain. I have aimed as much as I could at living a "good life" and have been blessed too many ways to count by God. Along the way I have tried to spread the word about offering up the suffering connected to a disability as a gift to God on behalf of others in books I have written like "Offering It Up for Souls and the World" and "Suffering and Spirituality: My Story."

Suffering is a subject most people prefer not to talk or think about, but like death, there are always those funny moments like watching my aunt stick a cigar in her husband's mouth as he lay in his casket and toasted him with a Kentucky bourbon and water. A sense of humor like my aunt's led me to write "My Funny Toilet Tales" about all the many humorous things that have happened to me like the time a woman reported me to a security guard when she found me using a handicap toilet facility in the women's restroom because the men's restroom did not have one or when a toilet broke while I was sitting on it, and I could not get off by myself.

If I could write a book about my life of suffering, so to speak, with toilets, I decided I could write about other connections to suffering like with healing as in the title of the book. I must admit in advance what started off on a serious vein went seriously haywire some where along the way to include the Wonky Donkey, Balaam's talking donkey in the Bible, then a U-turn to baseball and finally a camel for some unknown reason.

Hope you enjoy the humorous parts of it because laughing is good for us especially if we are suffering. As Madeleine L'Engle claimed, "A good laugh heals a lot of hurts. I will begin on the serious side."

Jesus healed many people when he walked on this earth.

A YouTube version by No Greater Love titled "Healed by The Messiah!" presents 61 accounts in the 4 Gospels of healings by Jesus. The Internet article "Overview of New Testament Healings" by Mary Jane Chaignot contains a chronological chart of the healings by Jesus, the apostles and disciples. The variety of healings is amazing including blindness, deafness, mutism, leprosy, impairments of the hand, legs, or feet, epilepsy, palsy, paralysis, dropsy, severed ear, insanity, fever, hemorrhage and a bleeding disorder.

When Jesus was not healing people, he spent plenty of time casting out demons and proclaiming the Kingdom of God. It is no wonder he was overwhelmed with all the demands on his time and needed to get away from it all from time to time. "Jesus left that place and went to the vicinity of Tyre. He entered a house and did not want anyone to know it; yet He could not keep His presence secret" (Mark 7:24). Jesus and his apostles were constantly on the go and found it hard to even have time to eat. At one point for Jesus, "because so many people were coming and going that they did not even have a chance to eat, he said to them, 'Come with me by yourselves to a quiet place and get some rest.' So they went away by themselves in a boat to a solitary place" (Mark 6:31-32). Did you ever want to think about what they ate on the boat? I'm guessing bread was the basic staple. We know ham sandwiches were forbidden but maybe they brought some smoked fish with them.

We can picture Jesus totally enjoying a party where he could unwind and have some fun after a busy day. He was relaxing and no doubt having a good time during the wedding banquet at Cana until his mother put him to work for a brief time turning the water into wine to save the family hosting the celebration from embarrassment.

The Bible says Jesus was invited by a Pharisee to his house for dinner. "A woman in that town who lived a sinful life learned that Jesus was eating at the Pharisee's house, so she came there with an alabaster jar of perfume. As she stood behind him at his feet weeping, she began to wet his feet with her tears. Then she wiped them with her hair, kissed them and poured perfume on them. When the Pharisee who had invited him saw this, he said to himself, "If this man were a prophet, he would know who is touching him and what kind of woman she is—that she is a sinner." Jesus knew what he was thinking, "Simon, I have something to tell you." Simon said, "Tell me." "Two people owed money to a certain moneylender. One owed him five hundred denarii, and the other fifty. Neither of them had the money to pay him back, so he forgave the debts of both. Now which of them will love him more?" Simon replied, "I suppose the one who had the bigger debt forgiven." "You have judged correctly," Jesus said. Then he turned toward the woman and said to Simon, "Do you see this woman? I came into your house. You did not give me any water for my feet, but she wet my feet with her tears and wiped them with her hair. You did not give me a kiss, but this woman, from the time I entered, has not stopped kissing my feet. You did not put oil on my head, but she has poured perfume on my feet. Therefore, I tell you, her many sins have been forgiven—as her great love has shown. But whoever has been forgiven little loves little." Then Jesus said to her, "Your sins are forgiven." The other guests began to say among themselves, "Who is this who even forgives sins?" Jesus said to the woman, "Your faith has saved you; go in peace" (Luke 7:36-50). The Pharisee was quick to judge and condemn the woman. Jesus was quick to offer forgiveness, grace and mercy.

The Pharisee was full of pride. The woman was full of humility. God resists the proud but gives grace to the humble. As the Good Shepherd, He sought the lost sheep wherever they had strayed.

Jesus was on duty at the Pharisee's house teaching those there and us about God's mercy and forgiveness.

We can imagine It was a different story when Jesus relaxed and had fun at the next guy's house.

One time when he was out and about Jesus said to a little man he saw up in a tree, "Zacchaeus, come down immediately. I need to stay at your house." As a chief tax collector, Zacchaeus had become very rich because he had taken lots of money from people unfairly. "All the people saw this and began to mutter, "He has gone to be the guest of a sinner." Just seeing Jesus helped to change Zacchaeus' heart.

"But Zacchaeus stood up and said to the Lord, "Look, Lord! Here and now I give half of my possessions to the poor, and if I have cheated anybody out of anything, I will pay back four times the amount." Jesus said to him, "Today salvation has come to this house, because this man, too, is a son of Abraham. For the Son of Man came to seek and to save the lost" (Luke 19:7-10). We can imagine Jesus had a good time partying at Zacchaeus' house unlike at the Pharisee's house.

Bars During Jesus' Time

The Bible never mentions the Jews having any bars or saloons in Jesus' time where the guys could unwind and have some enjoyable time imbibing wine together.

Jennifer Jordan writes, "There are approximately 256 references to wine written in the contents of the Good Book. From these references, readers learn that wine was made from grapes, figs, dates and pomegranates. It was often consumed as part of the everyday diet, during times of celebrations, during weddings, as gifts and offerings, and as a symbol of blessing." ("The Wine of Israel and Wine in Biblical Times", *Savor Each Glass*).

Excavations at Pompeii revealed meat markets, snack bars and "cauponae ("pubs" or "dives" with a seedy reputation as hangouts for thieves and prostitutes) according to Wikipedia. During Roman times, taverns or specialty wine shops (vinaria) sold wine by the jug for carryout and by the drink on premises. So, chances are, there were bars or saloons during Jesus' time in some towns he visited. All this build up leads to Jesus in a bar jokes.

Jesus walks into a bar.

The bartender says, "Let me guess… wine, right?"

Jesus says, "No, water. I'll do the rest."

Or,

Jesus walks into a bar and says, "Gimme a glass of wine, my son."

Bartender says, "Red or white?"

Jesus pauses, then says, "Gimme a glass of water. I'll decide later."

This next funny occurrence reportedly was a fact.

"When Romans made their regular visits to burial sites to care for the dead, they poured a libation, facilitated at some tombs with a feeding tube into the grave" (Wikipedia).

Here comes one of my all-time favorite jokes that is the basis for the title of the book.

A Jew entered a bar in a wheelchair one afternoon and asked the waitress for a glass of wine.

He looked across the bar and asked, "Is that Jesus sitting over there?"

The waitress nodded yes, so the Jew told her to give Jesus a glass of wine on him.

The next patron to come in was a Cyrenian with a hunched back. He shuffled over to a booth, painfully sat down, and asked the waitress for some wine. He also glanced across at the bar and asked, "Is that Jesus over there?"

The waitress nodded, so the man said to give Jesus some wine, "My treat."

The third patron to come into the bar was a Roman soldier on crutches. He hobbled over to a booth, sat down, and asked the waitress for wine.

He, too, looked across to the bar and asked, "Is that Jesus?" The waitress once more nodded, so the soldier said to give Jesus some wine "and put it on my bill."

As Jesus got up to leave, he passed by the Jew, touched him, and said, "For your kindness, you are healed." The Jew felt the strength come back into his legs, got up from his wheelchair, and danced all the way out the door.

Jesus also passed by the Cyrenian, touched him, and said, "For your kindness, you are healed." The Cyrenian felt his back straightening up, and he raised his hands, praised God, and did a series of back flips out the door.

Then Jesus walked towards the Roman soldier and was just about to touch him when the Roman soldier ducked away and yelled, "Don't touch me! I'm drawing disability benefits!"

There are many different versions of this same joke using, for example, a "red neck" or an Irishman. Sometimes it is an angel in a bar who does the healing, but I made up this version to maintain the theme of Jesus healing people like a guy like me as I sit in my power wheelchair writing this.

One more about Jesus before we move on.

Angel: Hey, Jesus! Some atheists are waiting for you at the gates of heaven!

Jesus: Tell them I'm not here.

"Out of the Mouths of Babes"

It is easy to make a transition from Jesus to Heaven, so here goes from "Out of the mouths of babes in Psalm 8:2 and Matthew 21:16.

Children's observations and come-backs about God and heaven can stop us in our tracks because of the wisdom they show. Only if we could be that open and honest without worrying or concerning ourselves that we might appear stupid in the front of other people or run the risk of offending them. The little children in Matthew 21:16 mentioned earlier did not hold back from crying out in the temple and saying, "Hosanna to the Son of David!" without fear of the chief priests and scribes.

We witnessed a funny little episode in our church on one occasion. Our friends were opposed to using the "Crying Room" in church. This one morning there two-year-old boy was acting up in church. His parents tried to quiet him down, but it was not working. Suddenly, his father picked the little tyke up, plopped him against his shoulder and headed down the aisle with little Mickey's face toward us. As his father carried him out, Mickey pleaded in a tearful voice, "Pray for me!"

The following is a wonderful example of a little child's insight built on imagination and creativity. The story illustrates how these special qualities show themselves in a child that has not been fully contaminated by American secular, rational conditioning:

"Melinda was a five-year-old sitting in a Sunday school class. Mrs. Snyder was the Sunday school teacher. The topic for today's lesson was "Love Thy Neighbor." Mrs. Snyder had a Master's degree in Pastoral Ministry and was considered a wonderful teacher. The children were asked to draw a picture showing love for your neighbor. Melinda was fast at work, hunched over her drawing.

When Mrs. Snyder approached her, she asked, "Tell me about your drawing, Melinda." Melinda said without looking up, "I'm drawing a picture of God." Mrs. Snyder smiled and said, "But no one knows what God looks like." Melinda kept her head down covering her drawing and said, "They will now!"

Mrs. Snyder then asked, "Can I see your drawing?" Melinda said "sure" and revealed her drawing. It was a big red Valentine heart. Mrs. Snyder pointed to the face with black tears in its eyes and a down-turned mouth of sadness. "Why is God so sad?" Mrs. Snyder asked. This was Melinda's answer: "Because big people don't listen to him."

Another time when Ms. Snyder asked the children, "Who wants to go to heaven"? Everyone raised their hand except a little girl named Sally, so she asked her, "Why don't you want to go to heaven Sally?"

The little girl replied, "My mother told me that I must come home straight after Sunday school."

On the very first morning of Sunday School, Mrs. Snyder said, "If anyone has to go to the bathroom, hold up two fingers." A little voice from the back of the room asked, "How will that help?"

Note the underlying freedom, spontaneity and innocence of the question from that little boy. As Rainer Maria Rilke, the poet, wished for herself: "May what I do flow from me like a river, no forcing and no holding back, the way it is with children."

How about this one?

Mrs. Snyder was teaching her class about the difference between right and wrong.

"All right children, let's take another example," she said. "If I were to get into a man's pants pocket and take his billfold with all his money out of it, what would I be?"

Little Johnny raises his hand, and with a confident smile, blurts out, "You'd be his wife!"

Little children can indeed be very literal. What you see and what you hear is what you get. There's no holding back as they can get right to the point. They tell it like it is.

"Grown-ups never understand anything by themselves, and it is tiresome for children to be always and forever explaining things to them", said Antoine de Saint-Exupéry.

This next little boy in his own way tried to get his mother to understand basic reality.

Marty had a little puppy named Pepe. He loved his little dog very much. One day Pepe became very sick so Marty's mother took the little pup to the vet. After examining the puppy, the vet came to tell Marty and his mother that little Pepe could not be saved. Marty began sobbing uncontrollably as his mother tried to console him. She said, "Honey, don't worry. You will get to play with Pepe again someday in heaven." Little Marty shook his head and said in a dumb-founded way, "Oh Mommy, that will be a long, long time from now. I'm only five years old."

One of my favorite church-related stories comes under the challenge of "My daddy is better than your daddy" heading that involves three little boys bragging to one another about how much money their fathers make:

First little boy: "My Daddy writes down poems on a piece of paper. He gets $200 for each poem."

The second boy says, "My Daddy makes more than your daddy does. He writes songs down on a piece of paper and gets $500 for each song!"

The third boy says, "My Daddy makes more than your two daddies together. He writes words down on a piece of paper that he calls a sermon. After he reads it in church it takes four men to carry all the money up to him."

Sometimes what comes out of the mouths of "babes" can be very embarrassing. Continuing with a "church connection", there is this beauty.

After the church service the preacher was standing outside saying "thanks for coming" when seven-year-old Mary addressed him: "Next time I come to church I'm going to have to put some money in the basket for you. "Well, thank you, the preacher replied, but why do you have to?' "Because my daddy says that you're one of the poorest preachers we've ever had."

As Oliver Wendell Holmes said: "Pretty much all the honest truth telling there is in the world is done by children."

As Mary, a 5-year-old shared:

"Each of us is special to God, so each of us should be special to each other. In a world where each of us is special to each other there would be no robbers, no fighting, we would be friends and play with each other and no one would be poor or hungry. I think that is what God wants his world to be like. I want the world to be like that."

God, Heaven, Angels and the Bible

Angels fly because they take themselves lightly -

G. K. Chesterton

God is talking to one of his angels and says,

"Do you know what I have just done? I have just created a 24-hour period of alternating light and darkness on Earth. That's good, huh?"

The angel says, "Yes, but what will you do now?"

God says, "I think I'll call it a day."

The angel comes back some days later. The angel walks into God's office after God has created the world and sees God drawing on his notepad a roundish thing with two eyes, a nose and a mouth. The angel says, "Hi God, what are you doing?"

"I'm working on the human being," says God.

The angel says, "But that's not due until the sixth day, today's only the third!"

God says, "I know, I'm just planning a head!"

Speaking of angels, a little girl was asked if she knew any names of the angels. She said, "I only know the name of one angel. He's called Harold.' Mommy sings to me the Christmas Carol: Hark! The Harold angel sings.

A little boy chimed in that he knows Harold too. My Mommie taught me the Our Father. "Our Father who art in heaven, Harold be his name…"

Halos

I have never enjoyed a "cutie", but I have seen them in the produce department at the local grocery store in a box reading "Halos". My immediate attitude toward them was "they are cute little baby oranges" and thought of them more like a kid's treat. This sets the stage for a wonderful comeback our daughter experienced with our four-year-old grandson Alexander.

When our daughter packed lunches for Alexander who was in kindergarten she was in the habit of putting a "cutie" also in the bag. One day when she was going through his backpack she discovered a number of leftover cuties. She said, "Alex, why are there cuties in your backpack?" "I don't like oranges, Mommy", he said. He then made a circular motion above the top of his head adding "besides I already have a Halo."

"Children live in a world of dreams and imagination, a world of aliveness. There is a voice of wonder and amazement inside all of us; but we grow to realize we can no longer hear it, and we live in silence. It isn't that God stopped speaking; it is that our lives became louder" (Mike Yaconelli).

Reverend Billy Graham tells of a time early in his ministry when he arrived in a small town to preach a sermon. Wanting to post a letter, he asked a young boy where the post office was. When the boy had told him, Dr. Graham thanked him and said, "If you'll come to the Baptist Church this evening, you can hear me telling everyone how to get to heaven."

The boy replied, "I don't think I'll be there... You don't even know your way to the post office."

Adults like me soon learn that children can, just like a well-trained parrot, blurt out things we wish we had never said in front of them. One time when I was running late taking the kids to school and was trying to put on my sweater while driving, I accidently honked the horn. The kids immediately asked why I honked the horn. I said, "Just an accident." Little Michael said proudly, "I knew it was an accident!" "How did you know?" I asked. Michael said, "Because you didn't say #XS*TZYB! afterwards."

The Bible features several animals including a camel and the donkey the latter known in the scripture most frequently as an ass. My favorite Bible story about an animal in the Bible is a donkey.

The Donkey

Donkeys appear a great number of times in the Bible carrying people or package loads. Two special riders on donkeys come to mind.

When Jesus triumphantly entered Jerusalem on Palm Sunday he was riding on a donkey. Not in a chariot or on a horse but on the back of a lowly donkey. That says a lot about Jesus and the message he proclaimed. Although he was and is Christ the King, people were not required to bow down before him. He was totally approachable by all kinds of people including tax collectors, lepers, Roman soldiers, prostitutes and people with disabilities, among others.

The second example comes from visual images rather than an actual scriptural statement. We can easily picture Mary riding on the back of a donkey as Joseph leads his pregnant wife on their way to Bethlehem where they soon would spend a night in a lowly stable at the time when baby Jesus would be born. Nativity scenes almost always show a donkey in the picture, maybe it is the one Mary rode on or one already in the stable. Maybe there were two of them.

That reminds me that many years ago when, early one morning, we took our little children to see a nativity scene on Riverside Drive in Covington,

Kentucky. It was so early many people probably were still asleep. We were whispering to one another as we slowly approached the exhibit. Suddenly, the live donkey brayed out a very loud "hee-haw" that scared us half to death. Recently I called our oldest son and asked him if he remembered it. He said he did. Then I asked him if we had scarred him for life and thankfully, he said "no". The little tyke was probably only five or six at the time. That donkey obviously was not asleep.

My favorite story about a donkey comes from the Old Testament Book of Numbers. The donkey's owner is a man called Balaam. He was a prophet who turned into a conjurer. In his time, the Moabites were deathly afraid that the Israelites were going to conquer them and appealed to Balaam to put a curse on them. Balaam was offered so many great rewards that he could not refuse the job even though God told him not to put a curse on the Israelites. Finally, God tells him to go ahead anyway even though he was dead set against it, but God always honors a human's free will.

We pick up the story as Balaam heads off to meet the Moabite king riding on his donkey with Moabite companions.

Numbers 22:22-35

"But God was very angry when he went, and the angel of the LORD stood in the road to oppose him. When the donkey saw the angel of the LORD standing in the road with a drawn sword in his hand, it turned off the road into a field. Balaam beat it to get it back on the road.

Then the angel of the LORD stood in a narrow path through the vineyards, with walls on both sides. When the donkey saw the angel of the LORD, it pressed close to the wall, crushing Balaam's foot against it. So, he beat the donkey again. Then the angel of the LORD moved on ahead and stood in a narrow place where there was no room to turn, either to the right or to the left. When the donkey saw the angel of the LORD, it lay down under Balaam, and he was angry and beat it with his staff.

Then the LORD opened the donkey's mouth, and it said to Balaam, "What have I done to you to make you beat me these three times?"

Balaam answered the donkey, "You have made a fool of me! If only I had a sword in my hand, I would kill you right now."

The donkey said to Balaam, "Am I not your own donkey, which you have always ridden, to this day? Have I been in the habit of doing this to you?"
"No," he said.

Then the LORD opened Balaam's eyes, and he saw the angel of the LORD standing in the road with his sword drawn. So, he bowed low and fell facedown.

The angel of the LORD asked him, "Why have you beaten your donkey these three times? I have come here to oppose you because your path is a reckless one before me. The donkey saw me and turned away from me these three times. If it had not turned away, I would certainly have killed you by now, but I would have spared it."

Balaam said to the angel of the LORD, "I have sinned. I did not realize you were standing in the road to oppose me. Now if you are displeased, I will go back." The angel of the LORD said to Balaam, "Go with the men, but speak only what I tell you." So, Balaam went with the Moabite officials.

You must admit that this was one smart donkey. His stubbornness saved his master's life. And as one observer put it, "Even a jackass has the discernment to not stand against an angel with a sword in hand!"

Also, don't beat a donkey that decides to talk to you. It may well be God getting your attention. Now you know that donkeys, at least this one, can really talk much less carry on an actual conversation.

Did you know they also play basketball? Yes, I have seen them play with my very own eyes. It's called "donkey basketball" that has been around since the 1930s. Donkeys gallop up and down the court with riders on their backs. The donkeys don't shoot but they can foul and fall over on basketballs to stop them from going out of bounds. Companies provide the donkeys principally for fun-raising events. They provide headgear for the riders, the referee and the game ball. Probably the best-selling point is "ABSOLUTELY NO AFTER SMELL!! Clean-up after our show is just like clean-up after a regular basketball game."

The donkey connection led me to my next association.

There is a very popular video game series called "Donkey Kong." I have a Wii video game my grandkids like to play called "Donkey Kong Country Returns." One time while watching them play the game I asked why I never see a donkey on the screen. "He's not a donkey grandpa, he's a big ape." I held back on a follow up question lest I interrupt the game again. I decided to Google it for an answer. My grandchild was correct, "Donkey Kong" is a big (King Kong size) gorilla. Originally, he was a bad character but later was changed to be a good one. I needed to know more why a gorilla was called a donkey. It appears that the guy who invented the game was Japanese and did not know the English word for "stubborn", so the best word association he could come up for "stubborn" was "donkey".

That got me thinking about donkeys in general. I thought about "Donkey" played by Eddie Murphy in the Shrek movies. After some time, "Donkey" becomes a faithful companion to Shrek, a big green ogre. But not at first. Shrek initially finds him to be too talkative and annoying but with time be begins to tolerate him. What I didn't remember is that early on, "Donkey" like Dumbo, could fly but not for very long as his power of flight immediately disappeared when the fairy dust that had been sprinkled on him suddenly wore off.

The donkey is the symbol of the Democrats. Thomas Nast, a political cartoonist, first published a cartoon depicting a live jackass kicking a dead lion in Harper's Weekly in 1870. Initially, the symbol was meant to mock and attack Andrew Jackson by his opponents. They insultingly referred to him as a "jackass." Jackson actually liked the comparison and decided to use it for his political gain. He used the symbol of a donkey or jackass as his campaign symbol.

What do you call a baby donkey?

A burrito.

What do you call a frightened baby donkey?

A chicken burrito.

What has six legs, four eyes, two heads, and a tail?

A man sitting on a donkey.

What's a donkey's favorite party game?

Pin the tail on the human.

What do you call a donkey with a doctorate?

A smart ass.

Who can forget another famous donkey, the "Wonky Donkey"? It came from a song by Craig Smith, a New Zealander who then made it into a highly popular children's book. You can find a wonderful, side-splitting video on YouTube of a Scottish grandmother reading the book to her little grandson that is guaranteed to make you laugh. It also has propelled sales of the book. I'll tell you how the book ends. He was a "spunky hanky panky cranky stinky dinky lanky honky tonky winky wonky donkey."

The donkey was "wonky" meaning wobbly or unsteady because he had only three legs. It took me awhile to connect to the handicap part of this book. Didn't it?

Handicaps

Here are two questions that start with the first part of a familiar adage or proverb and responses from children reported by a fourth-grade teacher:

When the blind lead the blind get out of the way.

There are none so blind as Stevie Wonder.

And now a couple of basic question and answer quips.

Q: Why did the man with one hand cross the road?

A: To get to the second-hand shop.

Q: How many blind people does it take to change a light bulb?

A: None, they don't need to.

A blind guy, a deaf guy and a disabled guy in a wheelchair pass by an allegedly magic lake.

Just for fun, they decide to try out this supposedly miraculous lake. The blind guy stumbles in first and stays around in the water for a while, then he comes out, bouncing with joy, saying "My sight has returned! I can see now!" The deaf guy went in right after and took a swim. He came out just as happy as he could be. "I can hear everything again!" The disabled guy in the wheelchair drives in, splashes around and then comes out, beaming and cheerful. "Guys, I have new tires!"

When my wife went back to work, I did all the grocery shopping. We have six kids so my cart when done was filled to the brim with mostly breakfast cereals. Instead of pushing the cart all around the store, I stationed it at a strategic location and then darted up and down the aisles in my wheelchair to pick up items and take them to the cart. A woman with a little girl maybe three or four years old sitting in a grocery car watched me as I flew up and down the aisles where she sat and couldn't take her eyes off of me. As I came back once again to her aisle, I was close enough to hear her say, "Mommy look at that man." Her mother shushed her to avoid any embarrassment but the little girl kept watching and talking about me while I was zooming up and down the aisle. As I was close to her, I heard her blurt out, "Mommy, let's get a cart like he's got" pointing to my wheelchair. Her mother looked mortified so I smiled at her and said, "No problem Ma'am, you've have a wonderful little girl." Mother slouched her shoulders in relief and said, "Thank you."

There once was a blind man who decided to visit Texas. When he arrived on the plane, he felt the seats and said, "Wow, these seats are big!" The person next to him answered, "Everything is big in Texas."

When he finally arrived in Texas, he decided to visit
a bar. Upon arriving in the bar, he ordered a beer
and got a giant mug placed before his hands. He
exclaimed, "Wow these mugs are big!" The
bartender replied, "Everything is big in Texas."
After a couple of beers, the blind man asked the
bartender where the bathroom was located. The
bartender replied, "Second door to the right." The
blind man headed for the bathroom, but accidentally
entered the third door, which lead to the swimming
pool and fell into the pool by accident. Scared to
death, the blind man started shouting, "Don't flush,
don't flush!"

Handicap Benefits

The usual connection of the last part of the phrase "I'm on disability benefits" is a monetary one like for the Roman soldier. It likely would be worker's compensation or a disability pension. There are other benefits of having a disability such as a handicap placard which allows the person to park closer at places like a ballpark, the shopping mall, etc. When visiting amusement parks like Disney World I and the persons with me are able to cut ahead in lines for rides and sometimes the ride operator would allow me to "ride again" because of the extra time it took for me to get off the ride to avoid the inconvenience for the able-bodied visitors waiting patiently in the long lines.

There are much more valuable benefits to having a disability like Helen Keller tells about herself. "I thank God for my handicaps, for through them I have found myself, my work and my God."

It took quite a long time before I could understand what Helen Keller meant. I was 22 years old and enjoying life to the fullest when a polio virus overwhelmed my physical abilities, but its greatest damage was to my self-image. Very soon it became obvious to me that I would never be a Big League pitcher, run sprints in the outfield to prepare for a game, dance with a pretty girl without braces and crutches on or run up and down stairs two steps at a time. I had been dealt a devastating blow to my body but more so to my spirit.

Disability presents the first line of attack on the person's physical and/or mental assets and skills. The impact reverberates to the person's goals and sense of self or self-image. In my case physical paralysis of the legs knocked out my goal of someday becoming a major league baseball pitcher. So much of my self-esteem was invested in my ability and recognition as a baseball pitcher. Instead of seeing myself as a healthy physical specimen, I was now a cripple, dependent on walking with braces and crutches and later, a wheelchair user blocked by a set of stairs or other physical barriers.

My self-concept and self-esteem took a nose-dive as I watched the reaction of other people to my physical condition. They shared about their happier and more successful lives while I wallowed in self-pity, depression and hate toward being dependent on braces and crutches then later strictly in a wheelchair and needing other people to help me. Other people tried to lift my spirits but often said insensitive things without meaning to which only made me suffer more. I struggled with the standard questions of: Why me? How did I deserve this? Will I ever get better? Is this life worth living? What will become of me?

In short, the disability took away my sense of pride. I was no longer who I thought I was. Now I was faced with the need for major changes and adjustments in my life. Once I was willing to accept my altered self-concept as a person with a disability, in time I "found myself, my work and my God."

When I was a little boy, I went to Mother of God grade school in Covington, Kentucky right across the street from Mother of God Church less than two blocks from my home. It was a German church. Some older parishioners still called it "Mutter Gottes Kirche." A German phrase proved a key to my personal and spiritual growth."Was mich nicht umbringt, macht mich stärker." It comes from Friedrich Nietzsche and means "That which does not kill us makes us stronger." Suffering can make us more resilient, better able to endure hardships. Just like a muscle, in order to build it up, we must endure some pain, so our emotions in turn will toughen up.

God has graced me with the gift of perseverance. As James 1:2-4 proclaimed, "Consider it pure joy, my brothers and sisters, whenever you face trials of many kinds, because you know that the testing of your faith produces perseverance. Let perseverance finish its work so that you may be mature and complete, not lacking anything."

Perseverance is closely connected to grit. "Grit is having the courage to push through, no matter what the obstacles are, because it's worth it."– Chris Morris.

Grit in my case has become a passionate pursuit to share the truth of God's love, mercy and forgiveness and the opportunity for us to offer up our suffering to God on behalf of others for their conversion and salvation in spite of my facing many obstacles along the way.

There have been many times when I felt I was not up to the task, but I believe my guardian angel in those situations has prompted me to pray for God's wisdom and strength to persevere, nonetheless.

Recently I had the opportunity to help my 11-year-old grandson face what he believed was an impossible obstacle to overcome. He is a Boy Scout and was given the task of selling popcorn as a fund raiser for his Boy Scout Troup. With tears in his eyes, he said in front of me there was no way he would be able to sell anybody plastic tub containers of popcorn costing $20 a tub. I had to agree with him when I heard the price yet kept my feelings to myself. Grandma asked me to talk with him to help build his confidence so he could go and sell some popcorn. I practiced role-playing a sales approach with him and in time be seemed to be getting better remembering his lines but still I sensed he expected to fail as a salesman. I patted him on the back for at least trying and offered a punch line to practice on his way out the door. I must admit I did not have high hopes he would be successful although I tried my best to pump him up.

I watched as he pulled his canvas wagon filled with tubs of popcorn and away he went. I was in the back room when hours later I heard his mom hollering with excitement. Our Boy Scout was happy as a lark and claimed he sold all the popcorn. He was receiving big hugs from his mom and grandmother when I had my chance to shake his hand and then hug him.

Here are three of the amazing stories he shared with us afterwards.

At one house as he approached the front door, the little kids let the dog run out and the woman was yelling at them for leaving the dog run away. Our grandson chased the dog captured it and returned it. The woman rewarded him by buying twenty-dollars' worth of popcorn.

Then he said when he approached another house, an old lady was screaming that a stray dog had invaded her backyard and was terrifying the little kids. So, our grandson the Boy Scout chased the dog out of the backyard and shut the gate. The lady was so happy she bought some popcorn too.

The third incident really blew my mind. He said, "This one house an old man opened the front door and said gruffly, "What do you want?" I said my lines and then he said what is your "sales pitch?" I told him what you taught me. I said, "You get plenty for twenty" and he bought the popcorn.

It was a joyous occasion as his mom, grandma, and I celebrated his success as a salesman.

Because our grandson played on a baseball team, and I love baseball this is the lesson from baseball I used. I asked him what a good Major League batter hits for an average. He said, "Around three-hundred." I said that means he is successful only three out of ten times. The other seven times he fails. That means he fails more times than not.

He said he understood and accepted failure is part of the game and realized some people may turn him down, but others might say "yes" because it is all part of being a good salesperson. That piece of baseball wisdom apparently lifted his spirits and helped prepare him for the challenge and he was successful.

The Spirituality of Baseball

In the movie "Bull Durham" Annie Savoy (played by Susan Sarandon) described church and baseball. She claims, "I believe in the Church of Baseball. I've tried all the major religions, and most of the minor ones. I've worshipped Buddha, Allah, Brahma, Vishnu, Siva, trees, mushrooms, and Isadora Duncan. I know things. For instance, there are 108 beads in a Catholic rosary and there are 108 stitches in a baseball... It's a long season and you gotta trust. I've tried 'em all, I really have, and the only church that truly feeds the soul, day in, day out, is the Church of Baseball."

Notice she never mentions worshipping Jesus. And a five-decade Catholic rosary has a total of fifty-nine beads. There are 216 stitches on a Major League Baseball, each side displaying 108 individual baseball seams. So, Annie has twice the beads on a rosary and less than half of the stitches on a baseball. But I forgive her because in her own way she elevates baseball to a truly unique status as a sport. It is not a religion, but it offers many spiritual lessons for one's life as I shared with my grandson the Boy Scout.

You can find numerous articles on the Internet about the Spirituality of Baseball. One of the best spiritual lessons centers on "home" as an analogy for heaven our eternal home. In baseball the object is to hit the ball for base hits with the goal being for runners to come home by reaching home plate. As a team sport, teammates help one another to get home as the goal.

I remember in a Catholic marriage preparation class a woman got up and said, "My biggest goal in my marriage is to help my husband get to heaven." It struck a chord in me, and I have made it the same goal in our marriage. I want to do all I can to help my wife and our children get to heaven.

Here are three of my favorite "quickies" about baseball:

Q: How do baseball players stay cool?

A: By sitting next to the fans.

Q: How is a baseball team similar to a pancake?

A: They both need a good batter.

Q: Where does a baseball player go when he needs a new uniform?

A: New Jersey.

The next ones get us back to talking about Jesus, the Bible, Heaven. By the way, I was thinking about how people seem to read the Bible a whole lot more as they get older. Then it dawned on me – they're cramming for their final exam.

Q: What position did Jesus play on his baseball team?

A: Pitcher. He gave his sermon on the mound.

Q: How does Moses make coffee?

A: Hebrews it!

Q: Is baseball mentioned in the bible?

A: Yes! In the "big inning"

Before getting to the joke about baseball in heaven, I'll share a true story about when I was a baseball pitcher. I later learned that a New York Yankees pitcher had said about the same outrageous thing I yelled one time at the Covington Ballpark to the home plate umpire. While warming up between innings I threw a pitch so wild that the batter in the on-deck circle had to duck. That is unbelievably wild but also true. The umpire took his mask off and hollered "Are you nuts or something?" I reportedly yelled back, "He was crowdin' the plate!" I have always been quick with a comeback. Please realize the on-deck circle where the next batter is waiting for their turn is typically 35-40 feet to the right or left of home plate. That was some wild pitch!

Baseball in Heaven

Two guys named John and Joe had loved baseball their entire lives and in their old age they would talk about whether or not there was baseball in heaven. They both agreed that whoever died first had to come back and give the other an answer. Joe passed away at the age of eighty-six, and John anxiously awaited for an answer to the question they had always wondered about. One day when John was sitting in his living room, Joe's ghost appeared and said "JOHN! I got some good news and some bad news! The good news is there's baseball in heaven and many of the greats are up there!" John was ecstatic but of course he had to ask Joe what the bad news was, to which Joe responded "Well, the bad news John, is that you're the starting pitcher for the game this Thursday."

One more baseball joke.

I took my dog to the local talent agent yesterday. We walked through the door, and I handed him our card. It read: "Barney. The Talking Dog."

The agent chuckled, leaned back in his chair, and said, "Alright, show me what you got."

"Hey Barn, how was work this week?"

"Rough."

"What goes on top of a house?"

"Roof."

"Who was the greatest baseball player of all time?"

"Ruth."

Just then the agent grabbed us both and tossed us out into the street.

Barney was just sitting there, looking forlornly at the ground and shaking his head.

"Knew I should have said Hank Aaron."

Well, doggone it, wouldn't you know that a talking dog would immediately remind me again of a talking donkey?

Here is a crazy story involving a donkey and the law:

"In the State of Oklahoma, it is illegal to have a sleeping donkey in your bathtub" (Rule No. 43, Silly, Wacky, Crazy, True Laws!).

Is it me or is that some goofy law? Why and how, in the wide, wide world of craziness, did this ever become a law? Well, this is how it reportedly came into being.

Apparently, a man had a donkey that slept outside in an abandoned bathtub. When a dam broke the flood swept the donkey and the bathtub a long way away into a basin. The rescue efforts were so costly the town decided to enact a law prohibiting donkeys from sleeping in bathtubs.

One can imagine the owner saying to the news reporter, "Don't blame me. I didn't make the damned dam break!" The donkey in this case made no comment, not even one "hee-haw." Back we go to other talking animals. In the 1950's there was a movie titled Francis, the Talking Mule. He was an offspring of a horse and a donkey as all mules are.

Then there was "Mr. Ed", a talking horse on the television in the nineteen sixties. He was a beautiful palomino that was described "as stubborn as a mule." He would only perform for his trainer and nobody else. He was trained to move his lips to simulate talking when prompted by a touch from the trainer that television viewers could not see.

I'm sure your thinking where is he going with this? Well, both of these talking equines, we can agree, could not actually talk in real life. They were great actors. But you already know about Balaam's famous donkey that could really talk that's in the Bible. By the way,

Q: What do donkeys send out near Christmas?

A: Mule-tide greetings.

Camels Apparently Do Not Talk!

There is another prominent animal in the Bible, the camel. There are fewer verses in the Bible with a camel in them compared to a donkey or ass. But there are several camel ones we can play with and several non-Bible connected ones.

There are two verses in Genesis involving camels that are easy to mistranslate.

Genesis 24:64 And Rebekah lifted up her eyes, and when she saw Isaac, she lighted up a Camel (cigarette).

(Genesis 24:64 And Rebekah lifted up her eyes, and when she saw Isaac, she lighted off the camel).

Genesis 31:34 Now Rachel had stolen Laban's household statues of gods and put them in the camel's saddle bags, and sat upon them and found them very uncomfortable. And Laban searched all the tent, but found them not.

(Genesis 31:34 Now Rachel had taken the images, and put them in the camel's furniture, and sat upon them. And Laban searched all the tent, but found them not.)

Actually, the second mistranslation is a clearer description of what really happened.

There are two more serious verses involving camels. The first one is about John the Baptist. "And John was clothed with camel's hair, and with a girdle of a skin about his loins; and he did eat locusts and wild honey" (Mark 1:6). A hair suit from a camel had to be pretty uncomfortable for John to wear especially in hot weather.

The next one is a very famous and profound verse in the Gospels which has led to various interpretations we will not get into. "And again I say unto you, It is easier for a camel to go through the eye of a needle, than for a rich man to enter into the kingdom of God. (Matthew 19:24).

Q: What do you call a camel that has no humps?

A: Humphrey!

Q: What do you call a three humped camel?

A: pregnant!

Q: Why do camels blend in so well to their surroundings?

A: They use camel-flage

Q: What did the camel say to the Sahara Desert?

A: Long time no sea.

Q: What's the difference between King Arthur and Cleopatra?

A: One had Camelot and the other had a lot of camels!

The Benefits of Suffering

Suffering can be offered as a sacrifice in life. A sacrifice is described as the giving up of something of significant value to oneself for a special reason or to benefit someone else.

The Sacrifice in Baseball

In baseball one of the special ways to help teammates advance around the diamond and on to home plate is to sacrifice for them. A sacrifice play means purposively giving up your opportunity to get on base to move the runner or runners nearer to home and score runs for the team.

A sacrifice in baseball is gift to the team to help them win. Jesus offered his horrific suffering up as a sacrifice for our salvation and to lead us to his home in heaven.

About suffering and sacrifice Victor Frankl said, "In some way, suffering ceases to be suffering at the moment it finds meaning, such as the meaning of sacrifice."

Suffering can be very painful but much good can come from it. Consider childbirth that can be one of the most painful experiences a person can experience.

"When a woman is giving birth, she has sorrow because her hour has come, but when she has delivered the baby, she no longer remembers the anguish, for joy that a human being has been born into the world" (John 16:21).

Women are willing to endure the agony of childbirth because it results in a blessed event, a baby.

It has taken me many years to accept the spiritual ramifications of suffering as an effective means of coping with the many challenges of daily life. It has radically changed my perspective about what really matters in life. Henri Fredric Ariel claimed, "You desire to know the art of living, my friend? It is contained in one phrase: Make use of suffering." A person must truly love God to be able to unite their sufferings with those of Our Lord as a sacrifice.

Suffering is mysterious, mind-boggling and like swallowing bad tasting medicine. But after many bouts of suffering, I have finally come to the conclusion that suffering has been good for me and God uses suffering to "perfect" us. "Sometimes God has to break you down to bless you up. Learn from your mistakes"- Unknown.

Here are several reasons why I have arrived at this point on the path of enlightenment:

• Suffering calls us to attention. If we merely treat the symptoms, we can miss the underlying meaning. It can be a prompt, nudge or a shove-also known as a "wake-up call"- to move us off dead-center.

• When things are going well, we rarely stop to ask questions about our lives. Suffering has a way of dramatically forcing us to deal with the deeper issues of life. It drives us to ask big questions like,

"Why am I here?"

"What is the purpose of my life?"

"Why is this happening to me?"

• Suffering seems to have a special ability to show us how much we need and feel compassion for one another. It provides the opportunity for us to draw closer to one another and to be mutually strengthened as we face the struggles of life together. Everybody hurts sometimes, and allowing ourselves to feel this universal emotion links us together in a web of compassion. As John Donne realized, "No man is an island." "And do not forget to do good and to share with others, for with such sacrifices God is pleased" — Hebrews 13:16.

St. Paul learned that there was great spiritual value in his suffering that he taught to others. As Pope John Paul II said of St. Paul, he understood the "salvific meaning of suffering." St. Paul wrote: "I have been crucified with Christ; yet I live, no longer I, but Christ lives in me; insofar as I now live in the flesh, I live by faith in the Son of God who has loved me and given himself up for me" (Galatians 2:19-20).

Romans 5:3-4 teaches us that "we also glory in our sufferings, because we know that suffering produces perseverance; perseverance, character; and character, hope." These qualities help us in serving one another. "And if one member suffers anything, all the members suffer with it: or if one member glory, all the members rejoice with it" (1 Corinthians 12:26). "For we are God's co-workers; you are God's field, God's building (of the Body of Christ)" (1 Corinthians 3:9).

St. Paul suffered every sort of pain, punishment, trial, tribulation, and humiliation. He never ceased rejoicing and teaching the spiritual power of suffering for others. We can learn from him that Jesus did not come to save us from human suffering but to teach us how to bear suffering for our own spiritual growth but also as a sacrificial offering for the good of others. "True and perfect love for the crucified Lord so esteems conformity with him that it regards suffering for God as a very great gift and reward" (St. John of Avila).

One of the greatest benefits from suffering is it teaches the virtue of humility. "If pain doesn't lead to humility, you have wasted your suffering." - Katerina Stoykova Klemer

Heading for Home

"My disability has opened my eyes to see my true abilities" - Robert M. Hensel

Returning to the baseball's goal of heading for home, let us turn to little children first for some of their views about home.

A new neighbor asked the little girl next door if she had any brothers and sisters in her home. She replied, "No, I'm the lonely child."

Pope Francis, during an audience in St. Peter's Square, said little ones are not diplomats and have not yet learned "the science of duplicity." And they let people know exactly what they are thinking, sometimes to their parents' chagrin.

A little family was growing bigger with the forthcoming birth of a new baby boy. Mom and Dad were talking seriously about needing to move to a bigger house. Little Billy listened patiently as his parents discussed possible plans. They noticed him shaking his head "no" slowly from side to side with a frown on his face. They asked, "What do you think about us moving to a new house?" Billy said sadly, "It's no use, he'll just follow us anyway."

A thief was committing a midnight break-in at a fancy home. While rifling through some drawers, he heard the words, "Jesus is watching you!"

He turned but saw nobody.

A second later he heard it again. "Jesus is watching you!"

Now he could see the voice was coming from a parrot. Relieved, he asked, "What's your name, parrot?"

The parrot answered, "Methuselah."

"Methuselah?" laughed the thief. "That's a dumb name for a bird. Who named you that?"

The parrot replied, "The same guy that named the Doberman Pincher behind you Jesus!"

Well, this writer, in baseball parlance, is "rounding third and heading for home" in the book.

"If I could make a cosmic deal, who would I put in my place? What in my life would I give up in exchange for sound limbs and a thrilling rush of energy? No one. Nothing. I might as well do the job myself. Now that I am getting the hang of it."
Nancy Mairs, *Plaintext*, p.10.

Like Nancy I am at home with my disability. I may still be paralyzed from my waist down, but the experience has led me to have a closer relationship with God as I hope one day to reach my final home in Heaven with Him.

I hope you have enjoyed this mixture of the "God teaches us" lessons with giant gobs of humor.

You will find some suggestions for offering up suffering in the appendices.

May God bless you and keep you close to Him as you make your way to Heaven as your home.

Opportunities to Offer Up Suffering

There are plenty of opportunities to "offer it up". Some preliminary points are:

• Don't pick something that goes against medical advice

• Select something that is easy to do that you are more likely to remember to "offer it up"

• It is awfully hard to think of offering it up when the pain and suffering are overwhelming

• Place a visual reminder of your plan that is easy to see, for example, on the bathroom mirror or on the dashboard of your car

It is easy to forget we do have a number of opportunities during each day we can use for offering it up.

Through repetition comes remembering. I have found the Morning Offering prayer to be helpful. It includes offering up our "prayer, works, joys and sufferings." At night before going to bed I review how the day went in terms of those four opportunities in the Morning Offering prayer.

Here is a partial list of some day-to-day possibilities for offering it up you might consider:

Waiting:

Waiting in the doctor or dentist's office

Waiting in line

Waiting in traffic

Waiting for a repair person to come

Waiting for a check or gift card in the mail

Waiting for a chance to talk

Waiting for the weather to change

Waiting for anything else

Irritations and frustrations:

When children are getting "on your nerves"

When feeling sad, depressed, angry, tense, etc.

Too much noise going on

When you catch yourself doing negative self-talk

When you have to get up and tend to a crying baby or children misbehaving

Certain chores like doing the laundry or mowing the grass, or other tasks you do not like to have to do

Biting your tongue from being overly critical or too judgmental

Feeling hurt, overlooked, not thanked or ignored by others

Listening to a boring or overly long homily or sermon

Interruption during a favorite TV show or sports game

This is a relatively short list. I hope you will find something you can work on. It is very easy in the beginning to forget. That's why it is important to select one that you are more likely to practice "offering it up" to accomplish your first success.

Don't get discouraged and keep the visual reminders in easy sight. With time you will build a habit of thinking about the first task you memorized and then you can confidently move onto other ones.

Offering it up can prove a truly valuable sacrifice on behalf of the beneficiaries and will make you spiritually stronger.

Good luck and God bless...

Other Books by the Author

Mary vs Satan: The Battle for Our Souls

The Pope and the "Sins of the Flesh"

Our Lady of Civitavecchia and the Bleeding Statue

Is God Using UFOs?

Our Mother Mary's Warnings at Civitavecchia, Akita, Garabandal and Fatima

Why Praying at Noon Is So Important

Your Guardian Angel: Things You Maybe Didn't Know

Holy Face of Jesus Medal

Evil Really Stinks

The Many Wounds Jesus Suffered

The Power of His Holy Face for Your Life

Thanks, God for Those Close Moments

LUST: The Devil's Favorite Sin

The Devil on My Shoulder

Growing Up on Rural Route 2

Sins and God's Warning

What the Angels Have Taught Me